OMF International works in most East Asian countries, and among East Asian peoples around the world. It was founded by James Hudson Taylor in 1865 as the China Inland Mission. Our overall purpose is to glorify God through the urgent evangelisation of East Asia's billions, and this is reflected in our publishing.

Through our books, booklets, website and quarterly magazine, *East Asia's Billions*, OMF Publishing aims to motivate Christians for world mission, and to equip them for playing a part in it. Publications include:

- contemporary mission issues
- the biblical basis of mission
- the life of faith
- stories and biographies related to God's work in East Asia
- accounts of the growth and development of the church in Asia
- studies of Asian cultures and religion relating to the spiritual needs of her peoples

Visit our website at *www.omf.org*

Addresses for OMF English-speaking centres can be found at the back of this book.

[faith >

in Tough Places

jan greenough

MONARCH
BOOKS
Mill Hill, London & Grand Rapids, Michigan

First published by Monarch Books in 2002,
Concorde House, Grenville Place,
Mill Hill, London NW7 3SA.

Published in conjunction with OMF.

Distributed by:
UK: STL, PO Box 300, Kingstown Broadway, Carlisle,
Cumbria CA3 0QS;
USA: Kregel Publications, PO Box 2607,
Grand Rapids, Michigan 49501.

ISBN 1 85424 585 6

British Library Cataloguing Data
A catalogue record for this book is available
from the British Library

Book design and production for the publishers by
Gazelle Creative Productions Ltd,
Concorde House, Grenville Place, Mill Hill, London NW7 3SA.

Contents

Acknowledgements

Jean Watson, *Bosshardt: a biography*, OMF/ Monarch Books 1995.

Eileen Gordon-Smith, *In His Time*, OMF/ Christina Press 1998.

The Long
March

In 1934 China was in uproar. The Communist Party had been increasing in power for some years, and the government was determined to crush them. The nationalist forces had encircled the Communist Red Army at their base in Jiangxi Province, in a siege which caused the deaths of perhaps a million people, through fighting, starvation and disease.

In desperation, the Red Army broke through the blockade and set out for Shanxi Province in the north, a remote and mountainous area where they could regroup and plan new offensives. Almost 90,000 men and women set out on this journey, known as the Long March, and over half of them perished on the 6,000-mile trek. The survivors included several men who came to power when the Communists finally won in 1949: Mao Zedong, Chairman of the Party, Zhou En Lai and Deng Xiao Ping.

Caught up in part of this incredible journey

was a little handful of Europeans, taken prisoner in a chance encounter with the Sixth Army. One of them was Alfred Bosshardt, and his courage and faithfulness was to have far-reaching effects on the future of the Christian faith in China.

Beginnings

Alfred was born in 1897 to Heinrich and Marie Bosshardt, Swiss immigrants who worked in a Manchester cotton mill. They took Alfred and his three sisters with them to Moss Side Baptist Church, where Alfred made his personal decision to become a Christian at the age of nine. It was a year later that a visiting missionary on home leave came to talk about the China Inland Mission. Alfred heard about the tremendous need of the millions of Chinese who had never been told about God's love for them; he heard about the mission which cared for bodies and minds as well as souls, running hospitals, opium refuges and schools as well as churches, and he was filled with determination to play a part in this work. As he said later, "The danger and adventure of a missionary's life conquered my imagination." In time, Alfred was to encounter plenty of both.

When he left school, Alfred took up an apprenticeship in engineering, but in 1920, when he was 23, he gave up his job and went to London to train with the China Inland Mission. He knew that many missionaries were gifted people with university degrees, and he felt commonplace by comparison. Nevertheless, he believed that if God wanted him to work in China, he would make it possible, and in 1922 Alfred left London for Shanghai. His early months of language training were demanding, with many hours of study each day as well as learning the customs and practical aspects of life in a foreign country. One of the principles of the CIM was that missionaries should live alongside the people they served, adopting the same customs of food and dress as far as possible, so all the students wore padded gowns and straw sandals, and were given Chinese names. Their aim was to build a self-sufficient local church, not one that was dependent on outside support, and that meant training local leaders to work with them and eventually to take over from them.

Alfred's first posting was in Zunyi, where he worked with other missionaries to teach and serve the people. These were hard times of famine and sickness, and the missionaries won many friends by their hard work and devotion, setting up feeding programmes and providing shelter for refugees. As Alfred's language skills improved, so his love for the people deepened. It was during this time that he met and married Rose Piaget, a missionary from the French-speaking part of Switzerland, and it was in order to be closer to Rose that Alfred added French to his language studies. It seemed a small, very personal decision – but God was preparing a path for Alfred which required such small stepping-stones as these.

Capture

On 1st October 1934, Alfred and Rose were returning home from a conference in the north of the province. There was known to be bandit activity in the area, so as they left Jiuzhou that morning, they took what they thought would be the safest road. However, as dusk fell, they heard rustling in the bushes. Armed men leaped out onto the road ahead of them, while others emerged from behind to surround them. As they were led downhill into a nearby village, Alfred realised that all their captors wore peaked caps with identical badges: a five-pointed star. They had fallen into the hands not of bandits, but of the Communist Red Army.

Both soldiers and prisoners spent that night in a large stable in the village which had been captured by the Communists. Slogans were daubed in large characters on the house walls: "Down with landlords and capitalists!" "Religion is the opiate of the people!" Alfred was taken to a house and interrogated by a man named Judge Wu, who insisted that the missionaries were really capitalist spies. The penalty for spying, he said, was death, but the Army had decided to be lenient. The missionaries would be fined 100,000 dollars each, and they must write letters to the Swiss consul and the mission headquarters, explaining these demands. The army had a long way to go and was clearly in need of funds. Alfred knew that finding such a sum was impossible, and in any case it was mission policy never to pay ransom demands – to do so would merely encourage every kidnapper in the country. He could not imagine how he and Rose would obtain their release.

The next day they were marched back into Jiuzhou, along with the army. The missionary house was attacked, and their colleagues Grace Emblen and Rhoda and Arnolis Hayman were also taken prisoner, along with their two children. At first, they were told that they could be ransomed for similar sums but then, unexpectedly, Judge Wu conceded that Rose, Rhoda and the children could be released. Friends with cars were able to take them away – Rhoda and the children to Shanghai and Rose to Guangzhou. Some days later, as the army marched onwards, Grace and their Chinese cook lagged behind and were able to make their escape, too. Only Alfred and Arnolis remained captive, caught up in a civil war and forced to march along with the Communist soldiers as they moved from town to town. They had no idea what the future held, and expected at any moment to be executed as foreign spies. Their only hope was to trust in God.

Loving the enemy

Mostly, the Red Army soldiers were young and fit, and they set a tremendous pace on the march, occasionally covering up to forty miles a day. Alfred and Arnolis found it almost impossible to keep up, and were constantly exhausted. Whenever they arrived at a new village, the soldiers would set about writing their Communist slogans on the walls. Next, they placed placards around the missionaries' necks and exhibited them in the main street: Arnolis was labelled "British" and Alfred "Swiss". Then, accompanied by music to draw a crowd, the propaganda squad spoke about the victorious Communist party and described the missionaries as imperialist spies, sent by their governments and using religion as a cloak for their activities. The people gathered around and shouted abuse at the "foreign devils".

Alfred looked around at all the hostile faces and reminded himself that Jesus Christ, too, was falsely accused and taunted. He looked from face to face, reminding himself that these were the people that for twelve years he had laboured to help when they were sick or hungry. As he gazed, he repeated a phrase silently to himself: "The Lord loves you and died for you." As he did this for each of his tormentors, he realised that he felt no bitterness or resentment, but only love for them.

One evening, after a particularly hard day's marching, Arnolis and Alfred were billeted in a Buddhist temple. As they lay down thankfully to sleep, a guard arrived and said that General Xiao Ke would like to see Alfred. Wearily, Alfred got to his feet and went out to the general's quarters. Xiao Ke was an intelligent and capable leader, full of high ideals and commitment to his cause, and Alfred respected him for these qualities.

The general had an unusual request. He had acquired a large map of Guizhou province, but was unable to read it. It was detailed and accurate, but written in French (probably, thought Alfred, taken from a Catholic mission); would Alfred be willing to translate it into Chinese? Alfred was taken aback. His captors were rebels, fighting against the government; they taught the people to turn against all forms of religion, denounced Alfred and Arnolis as liars and spies, and denied the living God. They were "the enemy". Why should he help them? Immediately, he knew the answer: "Love your enemies, do good to those who hate you, bless those who curse you, pray for those who ill-treat you." Alone of all those marching in this army, Alfred spoke both

Chinese and French: he was the only one who could help.

That night, the soldier and the prisoner worked together. The map was spread out on the table in front of them in the flickering lamplight, and, as Alfred translated the names, the general asked questions and made notes. At last, the work was finished, and Alfred went thankfully to his bed in the temple. He knew only that he had been obedient to the word of Jesus, but his actions were to have far-reaching effects. The general was deeply grateful for his help. Until then, he had been leading his army almost blindly through the countryside; now he could plan a route, avoiding government strongholds and heading directly for the towns he wanted to reach. He also began to develop a profound respect for the integrity of the two men in his charge.

A banner for the nations

Although the main thrust of the Long March was in a wide sweep up the west side of China from south to north, various units of the Red Army made numerous deviations to capture towns and villages on the way, recruiting for the Communist cause. Alfred was never taken on the main route north, but was forced to accompany the Sixth Army as they traced a zigzag loop in south central China. Often, their route avoided the main roads, struggling instead along muddy paths across the plains, or climbing the twisting, rocky tracks up steep mountainsides. When they entered a town or village, the army would take over the property of any wealthy landowners, killing their animals for food and allowing the peasants to help themselves to their stocks of grain. This redistribution of wealth was understandably popular with the poverty-stricken peasants: Communism had an obvious appeal when its army was handing out food. Then they held "trials", when the peasants were encouraged to come forward and denounce people for oppressing the poor, or for any violations of the Communist code of conduct. Punishments varied from hard labour or imprisonment to execution.

One night, as Alfred and Arnolis were preparing for sleep, they saw three terrified prisoners being marched past their doorway. A few yards further on, the men were forced to kneel down with their hands tied behind their backs. One of the guards drew out a heavy sword and beheaded them with three blows. He wiped the blood from his sword on the victims' clothing and strolled back into the village. Alfred said later that some of the army were "fanatics who would take a man's life as casually as a chicken's – ruthlessly dedicated to what they saw as honourable designs". The missionaries struggled to love both killers and victims as God loved them, as infinitely precious individuals, but they wept for the hardness of heart that allowed men to do such things.

Often they were joined by other prisoners, until they were either ransomed by their families or executed for their "crimes" against the people. Roped together to prevent escape while marching, the prisoners were intrigued by the missionaries' conduct, praying and praising God and singing hymns in Chinese. At night, as they read their Chinese Bible, the two men had many opportunities to tell their companions about their faith. Even in the worst conditions – hungry, weary, with sore and blistered feet – they were able to pursue their calling: to demonstrate the love of Jesus to the Chinese people.

All the prisoners were kept in the middle of the column of marching men, but they would sometimes hear the sounds of gunfire as the soldiers at the front engaged with bands of government troops. Then they would pass the signs of the battle – dead or wounded soldiers and civilians, the smoking ruins of houses and barns. Sometimes they passed the sites of executions: corpses beheaded or shot and left to rot by the roadside, bearing placards announcing their crimes. Alfred and Arnolis shivered as they recalled the number of times they had been labelled in the same way, and thanked God that they had not yet suffered the same fate. Trusting in God's provision, they thanked him every day for their continued life and the opportunity to serve him, and asked for his strength to save them from hatred, self-pity or bitterness in the face of all this horror.

One thing served to encourage them: they were told to march behind the standard-bearer. This man was entrusted with the Communist flag, a bright red rectangle, inset with a black star surrounding a hammer and sickle. On special occasions, such as the triumphal entry into a town, this banner would be unfurled and held proudly aloft. However, most of the time it was kept rolled up and covered carefully. Alfred and Arnolis were amazed when they saw what it was wrapped in: an oil painting of the nativity, doubtless stolen from some Christian church, looted and destroyed along the way. As Alfred said later, "And so we followed the Christmas star, like the wise men, uncertain where it would finally lead us!" Their banner could not be unfurled, but they knew which star they were following, and this small irony delighted their hearts: it was like a secret sign from God to them, reassuring them of his guiding hand.

Brought to trial

At times, the army settled in one place for a while, for days or even weeks, making forays to surrounding villages and towns, and sending messengers to other places. Occasionally, this meant new prisoners to be interrogated, men, women, young and old; the new order had discarded the ancient Chinese custom of respect for the elders. The missionaries had to endure the screams of terrified prisoners being tortured in nearby rooms; some were strapped to chairs, and others made to lie down with their hands tied behind their backs, forbidden to move or talk; those who cried for mercy were beaten. Unable to help, Alfred prayed for "the peace of God in the midst of violence, derangement and hunger". He said it was "like hell, the cries of the tortured most distressing". Yet the missionaries were still treated with some humanity, in spite of the serious charges against them. They were sure that God's hand was restraining the guards' behaviour to them.

On several occasions, they had been told to write letters to their families and the mission authorities, asking that their ransom be paid, but they had no idea whether any of these were ever delivered. As Christmas approached, they despaired of any rescue by this means, and wondered when the army would decide they were more trouble than they were worth. Torture and execution went on daily all around them, and it seemed inevitable that their turn would come. However, they were not guarded especially closely: every evening, the soldiers gathered for a Communist "fellowship" meeting, listening to speakers extolling the virtues of Communism and singing Party songs. Their guard often joined in, leaving the two men in a room with a ramshackle back door nailed loosely in place. Hesitantly, they began to consider the possibility of escape.

One evening in December, they slipped out and climbed over the back wall of the garden. They were free – for a while. Their freedom lasted only a few days; the army offered a reward for their capture, and inevitably someone recognised them and seized the opportunity to claim it. A group of soldiers soon located them and dragged them back to camp.

They were interrogated, but they refused to say who had helped them and which villagers had given them food. Then they were placed under close guard, with their hands and feet tied, and forbidden to speak to each other. At night, sleeping on straw and bricks, they had to ask permission to turn over; when they did so, they often dislodged the straw which covered them against the intense cold. All the time, they knew what awaited them: a Communist-style trial. They had seen enough of these to know the likely outcome.

The trial took place on Christmas Eve, in the market-place. The judges sat on carved chairs on a platform, and a crowd of soldiers and towns-people gathered to watch. The first prisoner was accused of hiding landowners in return for money; he was questioned, and the crowd asked for the verdict. "Kill!" they shouted, and the man was taken away to be executed. Then Alfred and Arnolis were brought up to be questioned.

They could hear the first execution taking place away at the edge of the crowd. Were they to be next? How should they answer the judge's questions? Then Alfred remembered the promise of Jesus: "Whenever you are arrested and brought to trial, do not worry beforehand about what to say. Just say whatever is given you at the time, for it is not you speaking, but the Holy Spirit."

"Why did you come to China?" he was asked. "To tell you of the one God and to call you to repentance," he replied.

Arnolis was asked about political matters, unequal treaties and the opium wars. He replied, "I feel ashamed that Britain forced the opium on China, and unequal treaties are, of course, unfair."

When the chief judge called on the people for their verdict, Alfred and Arnolis steeled themselves. Amazingly, there was silence. Then one voice shouted "Kill!" and another, "Beat them!" When the judgement came, it was a surprise: their fines were to be increased and they were to be imprisoned, Arnolis for a year and Alfred for eighteen months. Once again, they had escaped death, though every other prisoner called to trial that day was executed.

The next day, they sat in enforced silence in their cold room, each thinking of past Christmas Days at home with their families, and wondering whether their loved ones were safe and well. They should have been sunk in gloom, but they had been given the greatest Christmas gift possible: their lives. As he reflected on this, Alfred realised afresh that the message of Christmas was an eternal one: not just life in this world, but eternal life, because God so loved the world that he gave us his Son. He wanted to share this moment of joyful revelation with Arnolis, but he knew he was not allowed to speak. Taking some of the scraps of straw, he began to form it into letters on the floor: EMMANUEL. He risked a look at Arnolis and saw a smile spread across his face: he had understood.

I was in prison...

Unknown to the prisoners, the mission authorities had been working hard. Hermann Becker of the Liebenzeller Mission (an associate of CIM) knew General He Long, and wrote asking him to use his influence to release the prisoners. Three Chinese Christians took this letter, along with gifts and personal letters from Rhoda and Rose to the generals and to their husbands, and set off to try to reach the Red Army. On the first attempt they were attacked and robbed, but they persevered, and in February they managed to track down the whereabouts of the Sixth Army and follow them to Taoyuan. They had travelled for fifteen days, harassed by bandits, passing skeletons and beheaded bodies by the roadside, and fearing the worst for their friends.

The first the missionaries knew was when they heard the judge calling someone "the running dogs of the foreigners". Turning to Arnolis, Alfred said excitedly, "I think someone has come to find us." The following day they were allowed to meet the messengers. They brought them the news they had longed for: Grace, Rose, Rhoda and the children were all safe and well. Before they left, the Chinese men took off their shoes and socks and gave them to the barefooted missionaries; both men were overcome at this sacrifice on the part of their faithful colleagues, who had risked their lives to reach them.

The letter they took back with them to the mission from the Red Army was uncompromising: it demanded guns, medicines and money to be delivered by April. If this was not forthcoming, the prisoners would be executed. Once again, Alfred and Arnolis wondered how God could ever redeem them from this situation. Now that contact was established, messengers were sent to and fro, though not without difficulty once the army was on the move again. The army several times set dates for their execution, but then allowed the allotted day to pass without action. Reports reached Rhoda and Rose of their husbands' deaths, only to be contradicted a few days later. Everyone was living on a knife-edge of fear and expectation.

The mission still declined to pay a ransom, but

did offer a sum of money, ostensibly to cover the cost of the missionaries' food during their imprisonment. Messages were exchanged yet again – this time bringing personal letters and precious photographs, but still no money. On one occasion, Judge Wu ordered that they should be beaten in front of the messengers, to reinforce his demands; both men were stripped of their gowns, dowsed with cold water, and beaten painfully with thin bamboo rods.

Throughout the intense heat of summer, the army retreated higher into the mountains to avoid bombardment by government troops. Exhausted by constant climbing on the rocky paths, hungry, confined at night with other prisoners in cramped mosquito-infested quarters, both men became ill. Often, they were unable to eat what little food there was. As autumn came again, they wondered whether their strength would be equal to surviving another winter on the march. Then, in November, news came: money had finally arrived from Mr Becker. Alfred and Arnolis were summoned to Judge Wu, who announced that the agreed 10,000 dollars was only enough for one ransom. Arnolis was to be released, but Alfred was to remain a prisoner. The messengers had done their best, but it was not enough.

On the third day

Arnolis was reunited with Rhoda in Shanghai on 2nd December; his joy was tempered by his sorrow at leaving his friend alone to face the winter in the mountains. Alfred no longer even had a Bible, but his years of study were repaid as he recited the passages he had memorised. He relied on God's promises and trusted in his love, and sometimes his sufferings were relieved by unexpected acts of kindness. When the pain in his legs became crippling, he was allowed to ride a horse for a while; as temperatures fell below freezing, a guard gave him an old padded Chinese gown.

By the New Year, the army was moving southwest again, past the towns in Guizhou province, where Alfred had been working eighteen months before. His heart lifted as he saw the familiar landscape where he and Rose had been so happy. They moved on, keeping to the mountain tracks, into Yunnan province, and here, at last, came the news Alfred had longed for. He was to be released.

No particular reason was given, except for his Swiss nationality, and no money had been received from the mission. Judge Wu simply told him that when the army marched on its way the next morning, he was to be left behind. He was free to go home.

The next morning, Alfred awoke to the sound of marching feet. The Sixth Army was on the move again, but without him. After 2,500 miles and 560 days of darkness and pain and suffering, he was free. It was Easter Sunday, 1936.

Changes

A week later, Alfred and Rose were reunited in Kunming, and Alfred filled the weeks while he was recovering from his ordeal by writing an account of his adventures, published as *The Restraining Hand*. Then the couple travelled back to Europe, where they stayed for four years before returning to take up their work in China in 1939. As far as Alfred was concerned, the episode was closed. His experiences had been harrowing, but by the power of the Holy Spirit he had survived; his trust in God's love and protection had sustained him. He had been saddened by being described as a "capitalist spy" and an "enemy of the people", but he was willing to go on serving the Chinese people and preaching the good news to them.

Rose and Alfred worked in the city of Panxian for a further sixteen years, and had the joy of baptising one particular convert, Samuel Tang, and sending him to the Chonqing Theological Seminary. During this time, the Communist Party grew ever more powerful, increasing the restrictions on the churches, forcing them to register with the authorities, closing the mission schools, and persuading Chinese Christians to recant. In 1951, the China Inland Mission advised all its missionaries to leave the country. It was a difficult decision, but the presence of foreigners was making things harder for the local Christians. Samuel returned to Panxian and was elected pastor of the little church there shortly before the Bosshardts left China for ever.

The move was hard for those who, like Alfred and Rose, had spent all their working lives in the country. However, the couple could not give up what they felt was a calling from God. They went on to work with the Chinese community in Laos from 1951 until 1966; Rose died and was buried in the Chinese cemetery there, among the people she had served for 44 years.

Alfred returned alone to England, expecting to feel like a stranger in his own country, only to find that while he had been away, Chinese had been flocking to Manchester to study and work. Instead of feeling lost and alone, he was welcomed warmly by the Chinese church there, who delighted in having a pastor who could preach in their own language. He enjoyed a happy and active retirement. In 1973 he published a second autobiography, called *The Guiding Hand*.

Meanwhile, in China, the Cultural Revolution had come and gone. The Red Guard had destroyed the four "olds" of Chinese culture, custom, history and education, breaking up the old order and sending the doctors and teachers out into the fields to labour alongside the peasants. After the fall of Mao Zedong, a new leader, Deng Xioping, introduced a new wave of changes, reinstating the intellectuals and bringing in educational and social reforms. After over twenty years of being effectively closed to Europeans,

China was a mystery. Could the church have survived all those years of Communist atheism?

Aftermath

In 1984, a historian named Harrison Salisbury was doing research for a book on the Long March. He wrote to General Xiao Ke, asking about the prisoner who had translated the maps for him. The general told him the story, and asked him to convey his greetings to the missionary, if he was still alive. Salisbury sent the general a copy of *The Guiding Hand*, and Alfred and the general began to exchange letters. Alfred was delighted to make contact with the oldest surviving general of the Long March, and even more delighted to receive a book bearing the inscription, "To Mr Bosshardt, the Old Friend of the Chinese people". After being denounced as a spy and an enemy, being reinstated as a friend of the people he so loved brought him great pleasure. But God had further surprises in store for him.

When he had read Alfred's autobiography, General Xiao Ke arranged for it to be translated into Chinese and published; it was subsequently used as a history textbook at the Beijing National

Defence University. It bore a foreword by the general, admitting that the Red Army made mistakes in their treatment of the missionaries. He explained that his initial ideas about them were changed by Alfred's willingness to help him:

> We had many discussions together...all this brought us to a better understanding.... Although we detained Mr Bosshardt, he held no grudges against us. We should admire his heart and attitude and value our contact with him.

It is an extraordinary example of the working out of God's purpose that over 50 years after the rise of Communism in China, and in an avowedly atheist regime, a book should be published bearing the subtitle *Captivity and Answered Prayer in China*.

A further joy awaited Alfred. In 1991 he heard from Minnie Kent, who had been involved with the struggling little church in Panxian in 1951. She had heard, for the first time in forty years, from Samuel Tang. "When we left, there was a well organised church of 70 baptised members. Samuel reports that now there are 100 churches in his large area and 10,000 believers. More than we asked or thought!"

Alfred died in 1993, having seen his work in China come full circle. Through his obedience, courage and love, doors were opened for the preaching of the word of God some 50 years later. As he said himself, "I've always believed I was led along a path that was prepared for me. I always felt I had the comfort of God's promise never to leave me nor forsake me." He recalled God's word to Joshua, another courageous traveller: "I will never leave you nor forsake you.... Be strong and courageous. Do not be terrified; do not be discouraged, for the Lord your God will be with you wherever you go" (Joshua 1:5,9).

Alfred's steadfast courage had produced a bountiful harvest.

The Fat Cows
of Java

Fiona was lying very still now. The diarrhoea and vomiting that had racked her small body for days had stopped, except when her parents tried to feed her sips of water, when she would retch weakly. Her light hair was plastered to her forehead, and her blue eyes, which had been bright with fever, were dull and sunken, and rimmed with a strange black edge. She seemed to be too weak to cry.

Her parents, St John and Eleanor Perry, sat beside her bed and prayed. They could see only too well how much their daughter had changed, because her twin, Alison, was playing quietly on the floor beside them, a picture of what Fiona should be: bright, rosy and energetic. An illness which in England would be only a passing concern for a four-year-old had turned, in Indonesia, into a life-threatening nightmare.

The family had left England a year earlier, travelling initially to Singapore for an OMF orientation course and then to Bandung in Indonesia for some language study. They had finally moved to Salatiga in central Java, where St John was to take up a post at the counselling centre at the university. Now they felt suddenly isolated: they knew no doctor within reach, their grasp of the language was still not fluent, and they had no close friends to call on for help. Their only hope was the very basic advice they had been given on the orientation course: in the case of dehydration, feed a child Sprite or 7-Up, because both drinks have the right proportion of sugar and water to replenish lost fluids.

They spent an increasingly anxious few days, feeding Fiona with fizzy drinks from a teaspoon, until she suddenly began to drink, and to keep the liquids down. A week later, a medical friend of St John's sent them one of the UNICEF packs of proper rehydration salts, with a measuring spoon, to provide the correct treatment, but by then she was fully recovered. Her parents were shaken, though: they had brought their children thousands of miles from home, to a place where serious tropical illnesses were an everyday occurrence, and Fiona had almost died from a simple tummy upset. Their third child was due in a few months' time, and Eleanor was planning to go to a local clinic for the birth. Was any of this wise? Was it really sensible to expose your children to medical risks of this nature? Were they, in fact, right to believe that God had called them to the mission field?

Those he called

St John Perry attended his first OMF conference while he was at Aberdeen University. He got on the conference bus not to volunteer, but to argue with the missionaries: as a psychology student, he felt that missions interfered with the academic study of tribal peoples. However, he was surprised to be faced with two very attractive girls from the Philippines, who definitely did not fit his image of a traditional missionary. They pointed out to him that missions needed men: in many societies the opinion-formers were men, and it was often much easier for men to obtain a hearing in those cultures than for women. It was a challenging thought.

St John's own spiritual life was revived at that conference, and he began to think for the first time about the possibility that he might be called to do God's work on the mission field. He was in many ways a most reluctant missionary: coming from a non-Christian background, he met with considerable opposition from his family; his father, particularly, thought that missionaries were parasites who spent the money that other people earned.

However, OMF kept coming back into St John's life, and a series of events confirmed his feeling that he was called. On one occasion he wandered into a church in London at random, and found himself sitting next to the man who had organised the exodus of CIM missionaries from Hong Kong. When he took his first job after graduating – as an industrial psychologist at Rowntree Macintosh in York – his digs were in a tiny house close to the local Anglican church. On his first night, his landlord, who happened to be the churchwarden, said to him, "You aren't planning to stay in industry for ever, are you? What are you going to do with your life?"

St John replied, rather hesitantly, that he felt that God had called him to the mission field. The churchwarden looked entirely unsurprised by this, and merely replied, "Which missionary society?"

"OMF," replied St John, not at all sure whether anyone would have heard of it.

"And which country do you want to work in?" was the next question.

"The Philippines."

"What kind of work are you interested in doing there?"

"Tribal work," said St John.

"Well, that's very interesting," replied the churchwarden. "My brother is in the Philippines, doing tribal work with OMF."

It was such coincidences that encouraged St John to think that his sense of calling was true.

At around the same time his future wife Eleanor, when she became a Christian in Edinburgh, happened to meet the OMF Regional Director for Eastern Scotland. So it was that when St John and Eleanor married in 1979, they both knew that their ultimate aim was to join OMF, although at the time St John was still working at Rowntree, and Eleanor was a primary school teacher.

With this in mind, when Eleanor was expecting their twins in 1981, they decided that St John should leave his job at Rowntree. Partly, this decision was based on good psychological theory: keeping stressful activities in life to a minimum. Having newborn twins was likely to be enough of a challenge, without adding the stress of starting to train for the mission field. So St John decided to head back into academic life for a year, and study for a Master's degree at Hull University. This had the advantage that they did not need to move house, and after fifteen weeks of lectures he would be free to undertake his research.

First, though, he decided to check whether he would be able to return to his job if anything went wrong and they were not accepted by OMF. He expected to encounter scepticism from the personnel director of this large multi-national company when he admitted that he was planning to become a missionary. To his astonishment, the man said, "I want to tell you something: I'm a Quaker. During the Second World War I was in China, and I felt called to be a missionary there. But I never followed it up, and I never went back, and I have regretted it every day since then. I won't do anything to make you regret your decision as I have done."

Once again, St John was assured that his path was being prepared by God.

For his research, St John was offered a project sponsored by the Health and Safety Executive, who wished to discover the reasons for the high numbers of accidents on farms. A range of possibilities were being investigated, from the design of buildings through animal behaviour to human factors, and so a multidisciplinary team was assembled, including surveyors, architects, veterinarians, agriculturalists and psychologists. St John's research indicated that most accidents involving animals took place during the handling of cows – rather than horses, sheep, pigs, or even bulls. In order to analyse the human factors in these accidents, he devised some standard handling procedures, and spent a great deal of time observing stockmen on farms around Aberdeen, photographing, timing and interviewing them.

He became an expert in the kinds of accidents which happen most commonly. For instance, many stockmen lose all or part of the outer three fingers on one hand. This is caused by having a halter on a cow to hold it still for some procedure (such as artificial insemination, injection or taking a blood sample), and passing the rope around a post and then holding it. The cow moves, the rope runs out round the post and the stockman's fingers are trapped between the rope and the post. The simple remedy is to take two turns of rope around the post, which provides enough purchase to hold the cow without the rope slipping.

Other common injuries were blindness, caused by a cow's dirty tail flicking into the stockman's eye (remedy: hold the tail in one hand), and broken legs caused by a cow's kick (remedy: stand behind the cow – cows kick sideways; horses kick backwards). The next stage was to help farmers to analyse which people were least likely to be injured. The answer lay in interviewing people when they applied for jobs and assessing them for "trainability" – whether they would learn, remember and apply these simple lessons in animal handling.

St John enjoyed his research immensely, although it was very unusual for a psychologist to become an expert in animal as well as human behaviour. As he says: "At the end of that year I knew an awful lot about cows; I just didn't know how they could be used by God."

Mixed messages

In the autumn of 1982, St John and Eleanor, with their year-old twins, embarked on a two-year course of training at Lebanon Missionary Bible College, Berwick-upon-Tweed, with Eleanor studying part time. Among their tutors there were Frank Snow and his wife Cathy, the daughter of J. O. Fraser, the famous CIM missionary to China. By this time the two students were well-known to OMF, and had explained that St John felt called to mission in the Philippines, while Eleanor had an interest in Taiwan. OMF had considered the matter and suggested a compromise: Japan. A rehabilitation unit for alcoholics in Sapporo needed a psychologist, and as St John had done a special study of alcoholism as an undergraduate, he was well equipped for the task. The Perrys had accepted this, with some delight on St John's part, as he was looking forward to the opportunities for skiing in northern Japan. The Snows had other ideas, however. They knew of someone else who was equally well suited to the Sapporo post, and they suggested an alternative: student work in Indonesia.

All this was more than a little confusing: St John had somehow expected that he would have a clear direction to a certain area, not a string of mind-changes and compromises. However, the one thing that was clear to both of them was that they were called to OMF, and would work wherever they were needed. When they left the Bible college in the summer of 1984, they went back to York to work for six months in their old church, St Barnabas, to gain some experience in pastoring. Then, at last, they set off for Singapore the following January, for their ten-week orientation course. While they were there, the final decision was made: they would be going to Indonesia.

There are more than 20 provinces with over 13,500 islands between them in Indonesia, with a complex mix of 300 languages and 350 ethnic groups, and a range of religions. There are many nominal Christians, mainly because the compulsory identity card must indicate one of five religions: Islam, Christianity, Roman Catholicism, Buddhism and Hinduism. For those who have little interest in religion, Christianity is a popular option: it has no dietary restrictions, and there is no requirement for regular attendance at the mosque! To work in such a complex and hetero-geneous society, the Perrys were going to need every minute of the planned year of language and cultural study.

They arrived in Indonesia in April 1985 and spent two days in the mission home in Jakarta. It was an inauspicious start: the canal near the house smelt like a sewer and looked like black treacle – not a tropical paradise where the children could play but a squalid nightmare. They were relieved to move on to the language school in the high-lands, though the journey was terrifying. Their driver, anxious to complete the trip there and back in one day, drove at high speed through the mountains, overtaking on blind bends and screeching round the corners. The children were desperately car-sick in the back. Even when they arrived, thankful to have escaped without acci-dent, their situation was not easy. They shared their accommodation with a single lady mission-ary, who was heavily involved in student work. They were expected to settle in and be very quiet so as not to disturb her work – not an easy task with two three-year-olds.

Nevertheless, they did their best, knowing

how important it was to gain some language skills. They were learning Indonesian, the official language of the country, though they were to work in central Java, where many people also spoke Javanese. Their official role was not a missionary one. St John was employed primarily as a professional psychologist at the university; it was his missionary task to live out the claims of the gospel, and work among the local Christians, encouraging them to undertake evangelism among their own people. He says:

> Evangelism is about two things: proclamation and affirmation. In a "closed" country like Indonesia, the role of the missionary is one of affirmation, demonstrating the truth of the gospel, and then encouraging the local church to become strong and lively enough to undertake the task of proclamation.

St John was employed at Satya Wacana Christian University, in the lovely hill town of Salatiga. The university had some 5,000 students and ten counsellors, who worked in a purpose-built counselling centre on the campus. St John was the only foreigner in this work, and he found that he was a popular choice among the students who came for counselling. He suspected that this was because whatever problems they chose to talk about – sex, money, religion – they could always deny these problems later, and blame the confusion on St John's failure to understand the language. He also taught courses in the teacher training faculty, English for Business, and Management Psychology in Economics. All this was demanding and exciting, and his language skills improved dramatically.

Dark days

For St John, life at work was stimulating, but exhausting. On the whole, he enjoyed his work, but he found the theology of the Christian university difficult. The staff there had been influenced by a strange system of teaching on "Body, Mind and Spirit". This instructed that the three elements must be kept separate: the pastor had to remain off the campus, because his area of activity was the spirit, and that belonged in church. The university was for the mind, and so only academic subjects could be studied (theology was firmly confined to the theology department).

The International Fellowship of Evangelical Students had been ejected from the university, too. Both the Perrys were very uncomfortable with the difficulty this brought to student work.

St John found that working for most of the day in Indonesian was tiring, though it developed his fluency in the language. He was also taking a turn at preaching and teaching in the local church (and doing his best to avoid the contentious Body, Mind and Spirit issues), and since it was the law that all preaching must be conducted in Indonesian, here too he was on secure territory. However, in Central Java most people's first language is Javanese, and so in any informal gathering, in coffee breaks at the university or at church meetings, people would speak Javanese to each other, leaving him stranded and unable to understand or communicate. At home, Eleanor had the same problem: she could not understand her neighbours talking in the street or in the shops.

Then there were the medical challenges of living in Java. It was clear that Fiona had been close to death. What if it happened again? The nearest

OMF medical advice was several hours' bus journey away – not something anyone with a sick child would contemplate in summer temperatures of 30°C. Typhoid, cholera and dengue fever were endemic, and they fought a constant battle with the mosquitoes – what if one of the children developed malaria? In 1986 their third child, John, was safely born in a local clinic, as was Lucy, four years later. They had been advised against this, but their income was very small and the hospital was too expensive; in any case, they wanted to do the same as the local people, and not be different in any way. It was only afterwards that they discovered that a missionary couple before them had made the same decision, and their baby had died. It was clear that it was only too easy to take medical decisions which could go terribly wrong.

Eleanor, meanwhile, was struggling with her own problems. With St John working all day at the university and preaching and teaching on Sundays, he was kept very busy. She, on the other hand, found that she had too little to do, and time passed very slowly. She had been trained as a primary school teacher, but she was unable to teach in Indonesia: their permit stated explicitly that she should not work, and OMF had asked them to take care that she took on no responsibilities, as that could give the authorities a reason to expel them. They had deliberately postponed their training at Bible school until after the birth of the twins, so that Eleanor could take part: she was called to be a missionary in her own right. However, the difficulty of not speaking the informal language of the people around her hampered her efforts to get to know any of the neighbours.

The normal arrangements of life on the campus had ensured that she had some help in the house. This was welcome in the intense heat of Java, which made housework an exhausting chore, but it added to her feeling that she had no real role – not even that of a housewife. She cared for the children and taught them, but that alone was not completely fulfilling for someone who felt called to the mission field and wanted to work for God in reaching the people around her. She was even deprived of her music: her beloved cello had been left at home, because the tropical climate would have destroyed it.

Later on, when the twins, not quite six years

old, went off to boarding-school, they flew unaccompanied to Malaysia, to be taken on to school by people they had never met. With only one public telephone in the whole town of Salatiga, there was no chance of making easy contact; it was three weeks later when the letter arrived, telling their parents that they had arrived safely. The pain of their departure was so acute that it was days before Eleanor could go into their room without crying. In fact, this never seemed to get easier: they knew that each term they would not see the children for eighteen weeks, and for the first three they would not even know if they were safe. There was a long, eight-week Christmas vacation, then they would say goodbye again in February and return in June. Travel was so difficult and expensive, including an exit tax for anyone leaving Indonesia, that there was no question of visiting them during the term. Even though she still had John and then Lucy to care for at home, she felt that her role as mother was being eroded, too. This was another pain to add to the challenges of life at Salatiga.

Isolated, worried about the children, and feeling that she had no role in the missionary life they had chosen, Eleanor was finding their life in Indonesia very hard indeed. In fact, both the Perrys were feeling lonely. When they arrived at Satya Wacana there were five OMF families in the area, either working at the university or nearby. It had looked as though they would have the support of understanding friends to talk to and share with in fellowship. However, within three months, all the other families had left – either on Home Assignment or because their term of service with the mission had ended – and for various reasons none of them returned. St John and Eleanor felt very much alone on the campus. Like young couples everywhere, they were finding life with a young family very demanding and stressful, but they had no one to confide in. They had very little money and no car, so they were unable to travel to meet other missionaries on the island.

The gorgeous scenery surrounding their new home should perhaps have been some compensation: the hills around them were covered in rich, tropical green, with king palms towering above the coconut trees. There were active volcanoes in the mountains, and rice fields spread across the plains, dotted with water buffalo; not far away there was a vast inland lake. They saw glorious sunrises and sunsets, and enjoyed a tropical climate made more comfortable by their position in the hills: a fan was sufficient to keep them cool, with no need for air conditioning. Nevertheless, there were difficulties. Living conditions were more primitive than they were used to; there was only one refrigerator in one shop in the town; butter and cheese were almost unobtainable because they could not be kept; dried milk was the only available dairy product.

Shopping in the local town presented its own dangers. The campus was an hour's journey from the main city, but the buses were driven so fast and so erratically that the university staff had an unwritten rule: if a driver seemed to be more reckless than usual they would get off the bus and wait for the next one. One colleague did this one day, and, when he resumed his journey, he drove past the scene of an accident, and saw the wreckage of the first bus he had been on, with many dead. On another occasion Alison had a narrow escape when she was nearly killed by a horse-drawn cart clattering wildly along the street – she had dodged into the road to escape the attentions of a passer-by, practising the Indonesian custom of pinching the cheeks of children as an expression of affection. St John and Eleanor were very aware of God's protection at times like this, but with a young and active family, they felt hampered and endangered all the time by the difficulties of travelling. Much of this could have been avoided if only they had been able to afford to buy their own car, but their salary was too small. They could not mention this in their prayer letters home, either, in case this was construed as soliciting for funds, a practice which the missionary society did not allow.

In these dark days, both St John and Eleanor felt increasingly weighted by the loneliness, the difficulties and the dangers of life in Indonesia. The pressures had become so great that St John said, "If I had owned a credit card, I would have gone to the airport and booked a flight home." As it was, they were very poor – at one stage £4 was all they had in the world – and they felt trapped.

Above everything else, one thought was troubling them: had they been right to come? Had

OMF made a terrible mistake? They thought back on the mixed messages of those early months. Indonesia had not been the first choice of either of them: St John had wanted to do tribal work in the Philippines, and Eleanor had felt called to industry in Taiwan. Perhaps they should have been allowed to follow one of those callings – or even the second-best suggestion of Japan. There, at least, conditions would have been less primitive, with better communications, easier travel, and first-world medicine available. There would have been a more straightforward language situation, too. Never before had the grass looked so green on the other side of the ocean!

They had been well prepared for the trials of culture shock, a common experience of all missionaries as they struggle to come to terms with a different climate, language, customs and attitudes, but they had never expected that it would be as exhausting and depressing as this. Perhaps the problem lay in themselves – perhaps OMF had made a mistake in accepting them for missionary service in the first place. St John, as a psychologist, knew all about the necessity for rigorous selection procedures, and he had satisfied himself that OMF's systems were excellent. Yet possibly some error had still occurred in their selection; perhaps they were just not missionary material, unable to survive in this demanding environment. They both felt that they could endure a great deal if they were sure that it was God's will for them, but perhaps all their own prayers and testing and questioning had misled them. When they considered the tortuous road that had brought them to this place, with all its compromises and changes of plan, they were filled with doubt. Were they the wrong people, in the wrong place?

Pharaoh's fat cows

Reassurance was to come in the most unexpected way. One Christmas, a party was organised at the university for all the foreigners living in the area. Some were missionaries, and others were expatriates of various Western countries, working for international companies or government aid agencies. Many of the Americans were comparatively rich, owning cars and computers, at a time when the Perrys had never even touched a computer. St John and Eleanor were glad to attend because they were desperately homesick, and it was a relief and a relaxation to be able to speak English to others. It was interesting, too, to meet new people from all these very different worlds.

One such new acquaintance was a Catholic millionaire, a farmer from Minnesota. He came and sat down beside St John and said, "I hear you're a psychologist. You've got to help me. I've got too many cows." It was an extraordinary moment. St John sat very still, hardly able to believe his ears, as the party went on all around them, and the American explained his problem.

"There's a secret project up in the hills. The Indonesian government has to import all its dried milk from Australia, and now that the Australians have criticised the president and his family, the government wants to put an end to the trade. That means producing their own milk and drying it, and that's where I come in."

The Indonesian government had enlisted the help of the USA, and had brought over 13,000 head of cattle in specially designed ships. These had been carried in convoys of lorries, up from the port and into the hills where the project was operating. It was a large complex: there was a hospital for sick cows, and a helicopter landing pad so that the president could come and open the project once it was up and running. The cows themselves were huge beasts from the cattle-grazing lands of America, weighing up to 600 kilos each, and capable of yielding up to 30 litres a day when fed the right diet. They had been allocated to farmers in the region, six cows per farmer, and the farmers themselves had been gathered into groups of 20, so that each group collectively cared for 120 cows. Each group of 120 cows was managed by one Javanese boy, who had been trained in artificial insemination and relevant veterinary practice.

It was the largest dairy project in the world, and one that could only have been kept secret in a country like Indonesia, with its isolated villages and a government capable of enforcing its will. The rice farmers had been forced to grow grass for cattle feed, and there was so much waste product from the cows that the slurry was threatening the water supply of several villages.

The big American could see that he had St John's undivided, amazed attention. "Now, my problem is that the hospital is filling up with injuries; the boys have been trained, but they're not used to cows. They seem to think they're dealing either with a horse, or with a water buffalo – both animals that you can train and ride."

He took another bite of Christmas pudding. "Do you happen to know anyone who knows anything about cattle handling?"

St John swallowed several times before he could find his voice. "Well, as far as I know, there are two people who have specialised in cattle handling. One is Dr Martin Seabrook, from Nottingham University, but I expect he's busy at the moment. And the other is me."

It took a while to convince the American that he wasn't joking; in the end, he promised to show him his thesis with its photographs of "races" and "crushes" used to control cattle, the statistics and the lists of health and safety requirements, including suggestions for avoiding injury and the recruitment techniques for finding trainable handlers. He got the job: a few weeks later, he was giving lectures at the milk plant, demonstrating his methods on a model cow covered in carpet. The most amazing part was that all the boys were Muslim, and St John, a missionary from a Christian university, had been given the opportunity to talk freely to them in the middle of a secret government project.

Confirmation

For St John and Eleanor, the American and his cows were an answer to prayer. Suddenly, they had the confirmation they had been longing for so urgently. God had been planning far, far ahead of them: back in 1981, when St John had chosen his research, on a topic so unlikely for an industrial psychologist, they had been taking their first steps on the path God had prepared for them. It was like a thread of light, running from the carefree days of their early married life, with St John earnestly studying cows on the hillsides of Aberdeen, across the world through space and time to this strange party in the tropical night. That ray of light shone on their path and told them what they most needed to know – that they were walking in God's will. They felt, at last, as though they were following the Christmas star: wherever it led, they would go there, confident that God was leading them.

Their problems did not stop all at once.

Conditions in Java were still the same, and they still struggled with them; but the struggle was so much easier with that great burden of doubt lifted from them.

In 1991, they were transferred from Java to Ambon, and there, at last, they fell in love with Indonesia. Everything fell into place in Ambon: Indonesian was spoken everywhere as the people's first language, so they had no difficulties in making friends; the people seemed much more open and approachable; the church had a different style of teaching and leadership, with which they felt much more comfortable; and Eleanor found that she was able to take a full part in all their missionary work. Indonesia was generally becoming more Westernised, and this was reflected in many changes: Ambon had a cinema, and electrical goods like refrigerators were much more common, making a big difference to the range of foodstuffs available. The Perrys even had a telephone in the house, so they were able to keep in better touch with the children, and when the computer and email arrived, contact with the family across the world was possible. The old feelings of isolation and alienation were gone.

Unfortunately, the economic and political situation in Eastern Indonesia was deteriorating fast, and in 1999 all the missionaries in Ambon were evacuated; the following year, both the Ambon Christian and the national universities were destroyed. St John and Eleanor had to leave all their belongings behind, collect their children and return to the UK in 1998. They were very sad to leave behind the flourishing work and their many good friends in Ambon.

But OMF Indonesia continues. Existing church and student work offers many openings, although Eastern Indonesia, where Christians continue to suffer, remains in the news.

St John and Eleanor still feel great love for the people and the country. They learned many important lessons in those years, particularly about the grace of God, which met them at their point of need. Long before they found their most fulfilling work in Ambon, God moved to reassure them of his calling, working through the most unlikely circumstances: the fat cows on the hillsides of Java.

Perfume
at Bethany

For almost 50 years Manorom Christian Hospital has been serving the people of central Thailand, providing both medical care and Christian witness. Set among the paddy fields about 200 km north of Bangkok, it has been home to many missionary staff and their families, who live in the nurses' home and the scattering of traditional Thai houses inside the compound, and who work in the well-equipped 100-bed hospital and training school.

In Thailand, there are no general practitioners: patients simply take themselves to a local hospital and wait in the outpatients department (often all day) to see a doctor. Each consultation and prescription is costed, and the patient has to decide whether he or she can afford the treatment suggested. Admission to hospital can be expensive, as the bed and nursing care must be paid for, and patients' relations stay with them (sometimes sleeping on a bamboo mat under the bed) to help them and bring them food.

Manorom has an excellent reputation for the quality of its care. It has a long-stay leprosy ward, runs outreach clinics in smaller villages for leprosy patients, and it has recently opened a ward for patients suffering from AIDS. This is vital work, but at Manorom it has an added dimension. Jesus healed people, not merely so that they would become his followers, but because he loved them. In the same way, the Christian staff there work as healers to show God's love to the Thai people. They try to offer the best in medical work, as well as the best in evangelism, telling the people the good news of Jesus, and caring for their spiritual needs as well as their bodies.

A Manorom Christmas

In December 1977, there were three surgeons working at Manorom, together with their families and other administrative and medical staff.

Ulrich and Adèle Juzi were Swiss-German missionaries with three sons, Daniel, Jonathan and Lukas. Ulrich was the eye surgeon and hospital administrator.

Ian Gordon-Smith had studied at Cambridge and the Middlesex hospital, and specialised in vascular surgery. He met his wife Stephanie while working at Cheltenham, where she was studying to be a PE teacher. They had already spent a year at Manorom in 1972–3, and in 1976 they returned with their two children, Rachel and Mark, for a longer term. Christmas 1977 was especially happy for them, as they were joined by both Ian's and Stephanie's parents for the holiday; they themselves were planning to return to the UK a few months later. Their third child was due in February, and would be born in the maternity unit at Manorom.

Bryan Parry was a New Zealander; he and his wife Iona (always known as "Twink") had three children, Matthew, Rebekah and Adèle. As they lived in the hospital compound in the house next-door to the Gordon-Smiths, the children wandered freely in and out of each other's houses, and the families spent a great deal of time together. Twink was also expecting a baby in January, and the two wives were good friends; as Stephanie said, "Twink is always thinking of things to do, and we tag along."

Peter Farrington was a dentist from the UK; he and his Australian wife Rosemary lived in a house just outside the compound, with their two sons, Johnny and Ben. They also had a busy family Christmas, as Rosemary's parents had come to visit.

These families were at the heart of life at Manorom that year; the presence of so many young children made the compound a lively place, as they played in a portable swimming-pool and chased each other around the wooden supports under the houses. Eileen Gordon-Smith, Ian's mother, was impressed by the quality of fellowship and community which she found when she visited.

Her first impressions of Thailand were vivid and colourful: watermelons floating like green balloons in the canal; men fishing up to their knees in water; women in brightly coloured skirts and lampshade hats sweeping the road. Bangkok was hot, stuffy and noisy, and although they enjoyed seeing the Buddhist temples and the splendours of the King's Palace, they were glad to set out on the long drive to Manorom in an air-conditioned bus. The road ran straight as an arrow across the plain, with endless fields of rice on both sides, and coconut palms standing straight on the horizon. By the time they arrived it was too dark to see much, though the noises of the tropical night reminded them that they were surrounded by crickets, frogs, geckos and mosquitoes in large numbers.

The Gordon-Smiths spent Christmas Eve with the Parry family, singing carols by candle-light around the Christmas tree in their living-room. Bryan played the flute and Twink the harmonium, and the children sat on the floor or dozed on laps as the families sang together. The next day, all the families gathered at the hospital, and toured the wards, singing the Christmas story in Thai – for some of the patients, this was the first time they had heard the story of the baby at Bethlehem who was God's gift to the world. Then they went down to the river beyond the village, where five new believers were baptised. One of the candidates was a man who had suffered gunshot wounds some months previously. His face and jaw had been painstakingly repaired by Ian Gordon-Smith and Peter Farrington, and he had been so impressed by the love and care he received at the hospital that he began to ask questions about the message of the gospel. Now he was ready to join the little band of Thai believers at the church in Manorom village.

Later that morning there was a service in the little church, beginning with a nativity play performed by the local children. A visiting Chinese pastor preached on the text: "I beseech you therefore, brethren, by the mercies of God, that ye present your bodies a living sacrifice, holy, acceptable unto God, which is your reasonable service" (Romans 12:1, AV). It happened that the following Sunday a different preacher visited Manorom; he chose to preach on the same text. A week later, yet another pastor arrived, and the text for his sermon was the same one. Ian remarked, "I wonder why we've had the same text three Sundays running?" It was a favourite of Ian's; on his thirty-first birthday he had written in his diary that he was "a consecrated man offering myself a living sacrifice – my reasonable service".

In spite of the temperature, which was around 37°C, the Gordon-Smiths enjoyed a traditional Christmas dinner, complete with sprouts carefully conveyed from England by Ian's parents!

After presents and supper, when the children had fallen asleep under their mosquito nets, other missionaries drifted over to the house to talk and drink coffee and pray together. It was clear to Eileen that this was a very special community, bound together by ties of love and a common purpose. This and their faith, and their confidence that they were all doing God's will, enabled these young families to face and overcome the heat, the exhaustion, the cultural differences, the hard work and frustrations of missionary life.

It had been a happy holiday for everyone. Just after Christmas they were joined by Noel and Louise Sampson, with their two-year-old son, Ben. Louise's baby was due later in January, and she wanted to see the maternity unit and settle in; they were to take over from the Gordon-Smiths later in the year. By the middle of January, all the visitors had departed, leaving the Manorom missionary team, augmented by the Sampson family, to take up their work again.

Children's Day

Children in Thailand are considered the country's most valuable resource. There is a Thai saying:

"Children are the future of the nation. If the children are intelligent, the country will be prosperous." To show how they value them, every year the people celebrate National Children's Day on the second Saturday in January, by taking their children on outings to visit special places or just for sightseeing, picnics and fun. In 1978, that day was Saturday 14th January.

That year was one of major outreach for the Thai church. There had been a great deal of prayer and planning for a campaign called The Thrust, and many of the Manorom church were involved in visiting homes in nearby towns. On Saturday 14th January Peter Farrington was going to Paknampho, so Rosemary arranged to spend the day with the Gordon-Smiths. They decided to use the hospital minibus for a Children's Day outing to Phao-Ha, to see the rice harvest being loaded onto the barges.

They met at the Parry's house for a cup of coffee, where Twink said, "That sounds lovely. Can we come?" Then the Sampsons and Dr Julia Brown, a paediatrician, decided to join the party. Johnny Farrington was playing outside with Jonathan and Lukas Juzi, and invited them, and they ran home to ask their mother if they might go too. Adèle hesitated at first, because Ulrich had taken their eldest son, Daniel, on a ward round with him; she thought he might be disappointed to find that the others had gone without him, but eventually she relented.

So the bus set off with seven adults and ten children: full, but not overloaded. It was a beautiful day – the sky was blue and the sun warm, but it was not too hot for comfort. They stopped on the way to Phao-Ha to look at the threshing and winnowing floors, and then drove on to the river bank where the barges were loaded. Loose rice was piled in huge heaps, and being swept into wide baskets and carried down to the boats. It was a brilliant scene: the workers wore loose tunics and trousers, with wide-brimmed straw hats and bright scarves; they carried the baskets swinging on yokes across their shoulders. The children scampered around as though on a sandy beach, making their own little piles of rice, and scooping up handfuls to help fill the baskets. They were not really helping much, but the Thais love children, and were charmed by these white-skinned, blue-eyed children who chattered to them in their own language. Stephanie looked fondly at Rachel's dark head and Mark's blonde one bent earnestly together over a basket, and Rosemary took a photograph of Johnny playing in the rice.

Eventually Ian looked at his watch. "Time to go home," he called, and climbed back into the driver's seat. The others gathered up the children, some of whom had wandered down to the water's edge to watch the boats. After a while everyone was on board; Rosemary Farrington came last, and sat in the front passenger seat with two-year-old Ben on her lap. Then they set off homewards, rattling down the dusty road to Manorom. Noel Sampson leaned forward in his seat behind the driver.

"Thanks a lot, Ian, it's been a lovely morning," he said.

"We're not home yet," replied Ian.

Already with the Lord

The road was as busy as usual, and they were not driving very fast. In the back, everyone was talking about the rice harvest. Only Rosemary and Ian saw what happened next: a Chiang Mai bus came towards them on the other side of the road, and just as they were passing it, a large vehicle close behind it suddenly pulled out at speed and tried to overtake. It was travelling too close to the bus to have seen the minibus in the way, and there was no time to swerve: the head-on collision was immediate.

The impact forced the passenger door to fly off, and Rosemary was thrown clear of the bus, holding Ben tightly in her arms. The rest of the bus was crushed.

When Rosemary regained consciousness, she was lying by the side of the road; Ben was beside her, screaming, with blood running down his face; the agonising pain in her arm told her it was broken. Then she realised that behind the sound of Ben's crying there was a terrible silence. She raised her head and looked around. There were no other voices, and all around her were the bodies of her friends.

She managed to get up, and stumbled from one body to another; Matthew and her own Ben had cuts and grazes, Jonathan Juzi and Julia Brown were seriously injured but still breathing. Everyone else was dead, including her own son

Johnny. The driver of the other vehicle had scrambled from the wreck and run off, leaving his passenger behind with a broken leg. A crowd had gathered, and Rosemary pleaded with them to help, but the Thais were reluctant to intervene. They believe that they will be haunted by evil spirits if someone dies in their car. Fortunately, a young Thai man called Soomet got off a bus and came to help; he persuaded two of his friends who were passing in a Land Rover to drive them to the hospital.

Back at Manorom, Ulrich Juzi had returned from his ward round and was surprised to find that the minibus had not yet returned; Adèle was uneasy, and had already paused in her work to pray and commit her children to the Lord. Then the telephone rang, and she knew before she answered it that it was bad news. A Land Rover drove into the compound, and people ran out to lift the injured onto stretchers; Adèle ran to her car and drove out to the scene of the accident, hoping that there would be someone left alive that she could help.

When she got there, a policeman tried to hold her back, but she saw the twelve bodies lying by the roadside. One of them was little Lukas, her youngest son. She stood looking at him as if stunned, and then became aware of the Thai people gathered round. All at once she saw the scene through their eyes, and her heart was filled with pity for them. She knew that for them death was the end, and that when their loved ones died, they were lost to them for ever. In spite of the grief that was already gripping her, she turned to them.

"These people who have died are not here any more," she said. "They are already with the Lord, and they were ready to meet him. I have one wish – that you, all of you, will never forget this sad scene, and that whenever you hear anything about the Lord Jesus you will open your hearts to him, so that when you have to die you will be as ready to meet the Lord as these people have been."

Adèle returned to Manorom as the first of the dead were brought home; in her words, the Lord had "called the twelve unto himself". In context, these words from Matthew 10:1 refer to the twelve disciples, but since all those who died in the accident were Christ's people and went to be with him in heaven, the words held a special meaning for her.

It was a melancholy roll-call: Ian and Stephanie Gordon-Smith, six-year-old Rachel and four-year-old Mark, and Stephanie's unborn baby; Noel and Louise Sampson and two-year-old Ben, and Louise's unborn baby; Twink Parry, five-year-old Rebekah and two-year-old Adèle, and Twink's unborn baby; Johnny Farrington and Lukas Juzi, both aged five.

The path of life

In the early afternoon, Peter Farrington received a message that the minibus had been in a serious accident and that Rosemary and his children were involved; he and the rest of the team set off back to Manorom at once, praying desperately, and with no idea what they would find when they got there. On the way, they passed the remains of the minibus, completely crushed by a large van. He turned to the others and said, "Nobody could have survived that accident."

As he entered the hospital, he was aware that his fears were calmed by a tremendous sense of peace and the assurance that God, the loving

Father, was in control. He found Rosemary on the ward and Ben in the emergency room, waiting for surgery, and he was told that five-year-old Johnny was dead. Bryan Parry had arrived to find that his wife and daughters were all dead; his one remaining child, Matthew, was waiting for treatment.

Whatever their feelings, both men had work to do. Somehow, they had to turn their minds from the images of the lethal impact and buckled metal of the crushed vehicles, and from the anguish of their own loss, and scrub up to operate on their family and friends. Peter stitched his son Ben's cut head and face. "I was glad the Lord helped me to be a surgeon and not a father for that operation," he said. Bryan operated on Jonathan Juzi, who had internal injuries, and then stitched his own son Matthew's foot. Bryan and Peter worked together on Dr Julia Brown, who had multiple fractures, and another doctor set Rosemary's broken arm and dealt with her other injuries. Only then could they turn to each other and share their grief and shock.

The only survivor who remembered the accident clearly was Rosemary. She was certain that no one in the bus that day had any idea of what was happening, and in the second between seeing the other vehicle and the crash, there was no time for fear. She said:

> It's a comfort to me that our loved ones would have gone out as quickly as I did, but they didn't wake up to the terror and the horridness. It's a lovely thing that they went straight to the Lord and they didn't have to wake up to life with what was left. There was peace on their faces, and some smiles; it's a lovely thing, and we praise the Lord that there wasn't suffering.

Dr John Townsend was on Home Assignment in the UK, but when he heard the news he flew back to Thailand at once. He said, "Adèle's first words to me were: 'God is good.' Her face was that of Mary at the foot of the cross."

Somehow, those who were left had to make sense of what had happened; in the midst of their grief, they continued to work and witness to the Thai people. Three days after the accident, a memorial and thanksgiving service was held in the compound of Manorom Hospital. Hundreds of people came in from the fields and the markets to share in the service; some of them had worked late into the night making traditional floral tributes in silk and cotton. Schools were officially closed so that teachers could attend if they wished, and government officials sat in a row at the front. An address was given in English and Thai, explaining the Christian message of hope and the certainty of eternal life in the face of death: several hundred people accepted extracts from the Gospels.

On the following day, twelve bodies were buried in a communal grave in the Protestant cemetery in Bangkok, in a simple service. Everyone there felt the presence of God among them. Peter Farrington said, "I could only praise him through my tears." Later, the grave was marked by a grey and white stone bearing the names of all those who died, together with the words of Psalm 16:11 (RSV) – "Thou dost show me the path of life; in thy presence there is fulness of joy; at thy right hand there are pleasures for evermore."

Why this waste?

Throughout the years since the tragedy at Manorom, people have asked: "Why?" On a human level, the explanation is simple: Thailand is known for its dangerous roads, and traffic accidents claim many lives each year. Someone drove badly and made a poor decision, and the result was a serious accident. Christians may bring other interpretations to the suffering that resulted from this accident. Some wondered whether it was linked to the spiritual breakthrough in Thailand, towards which the missionaries were working that year; they thought perhaps it was the work of the devil, who wants to undermine the good work done in the name of the gospel.

This, however, merely leads to another question: why did God not intervene to save the lives of his faithful servants? Surely the one who holds the world in his hand could have worked a little miracle to protect those happy, innocent children and their loving parents? To this, Bryan Parry replies, "God does not have to justify to me, or give his reasons for what he has permitted." Ulrich Juzi spoke at the memorial service and quoted the words of Job: "The Lord gave and the Lord has taken away; may the name of the Lord be praised." These are, like the whole book of Job, answers which are not answers; words which do not rationalise or excuse, but which touch the deep part of our hearts in which we know that God is so far above our human reasoning as to be unknowable, incomprehensible. The only part of God which we can know is his love.

We know the love of God through Jesus. The idea of suffering which so troubled the Old Testament writers is transformed in the New Testament through the suffering of Jesus on the cross. His suffering is the gate through which we reach heaven, and Paul says, "Now I rejoice in what was suffered for you" (Colossians 1:24). Christians count it a privilege to bear his name, and know that "Whoever serves me must follow me" (John 12:26). Following Jesus can mean suffering, especially for those who follow him into foreign countries to seek the lost and do his will, to "make disciples of all nations, baptising them in the name of the Father and of the Son and of the Holy Spirit" (Matthew 28:19).

The history of missions is a history of suffering, and the pioneers who ventured abroad in answer to God's call before the days of modern medicines often endured terrible losses. Yet they laid the foundations of work which is bearing fruit all over the world today. They were Christians who shared in the suffering of Christ to save the world, and to bring the light of his love to people who would otherwise be in darkness. They submitted their lives to the sovereignty of his will, trusting in his love. In the words of Ian Gordon-Smith's verse, offering their bodies as living sacrifices, holy and pleasing to God.

It may seem that the young families who died at Manorom are lost to us, and that their lives, which could have been spent helping the poor in Thailand, were poured out for nothing. This was the cry of the disciples, when Mary poured out the perfume at Bethany and anointed Jesus with it: "Why this waste?... This perfume could have been sold... and the money given to the poor" (Matthew 26:8, 9). Jesus replied, "She has done a beautiful thing to me." What is given in honour of God is never wasted.

Bryan Parry wrote, "The Lord has proved himself to be more than sufficient to my need. His loving attention to all the details has touched me, too." To the families who were left behind, there were clear signs of God's love all around them. It seemed to them that the children, in particular, had shown signs of special happiness and peace in the weeks leading up to the accident. Eileen Gordon-Smith, who visited her grandchildren that Christmas, noticed a change in Mark, who had become "sweet and amiable, easy to play with and amenable to others". Lukas Juzi, only five years old, had been asking his parents curious questions about life after death; he had always been a happy, humorous little boy, but he seemed to be especially obedient, good and happy during those weeks. The night before the accident, Johnny Farrington had asked his mother what heaven would be like, and she tried to explain how beautiful it would be by showing him the diamonds in her engagement ring. "What will we wear?" he asked. "Beautiful, white, shining clothes," she replied.

Bryan Parry also had only happy memories of family life in those weeks. Twink had remarked to him, "Do you know, I can never remember a time when our family has been more united." He felt that God was not only preparing the children; he himself had had a curious dream one night. In it, he saw Twink and the two girls standing on a wide staircase bathed in light, and thought, "Why am I not on the stairs with them? And where is Matthew?" After the accident, he felt that this gave him some assurance that everything was part of God's plan.

Rosemary Farrington remarked that "the Lord ordered that accident in a lovely way". She noted that two entire families went together, and that of the survivors no child was left without any parent, and no parent was left without any children.

Bearing fruit

The accident at Manorom damaged both the people involved and their work. David Pickard was the Area Director for Thailand, and a close personal friend of the Gordon-Smiths: he and his wife had been baby-sitting for them only two days before the accident. David was faced with a daunting task, contacting relatives, consulting mission leaders, comforting friends, making arrangements, and finally conducting a funeral for twelve people. He was supported lovingly by his colleagues, all of whom were struggling with their own grief, and all of whom knew that they needed the peace and strength of the Lord more than they ever had before.

Other urgent questions began to present themselves. How could Manorom Hospital continue to run, with two of its surgeons dead? Surely no one would want to come out to Thailand after this proof of the precarious nature of missionary work. The answer to that problem came almost at once. Dr John Upsdell and his wife Alex had previously worked at Manorom, and were now living in the UK. They applied at once for permission to return, with their two small daughters, and helped to keep Manorom running during the next six months. At the same time, John Belstead, a surgeon, and his wife Sue, an anaesthetist, had asked the Lord to help them decide whether to volunteer for service overseas. When they switched on the radio and heard the news of the accident, they knew that they had their answer.

This was repeated many times. Out of the accident grew a community of loving friends who had grieved together and learned to trust God more profoundly. All over the world, people have heard the story of Manorom and dedicated their lives to God, and some have become missionaries in their turn.

Manorom itself has moved on, continuing to provide medical care for the people of central Thailand. It still specialises in leprosy care. Even though there are now drugs available to cure the disease, there are still many leprosy sufferers in Thailand, in need of the surgery and physiotherapy which enables them to overcome the handicaps resulting from their injuries. Often, these people speak of the love and care with which they are tended, and what it means to them when a nurse is willing to lift and bathe their ulcerated feet, when no one else has touched them, perhaps for years.

A similar isolation is now felt by sufferers from HIV and AIDS, who often try to hide their condition because they know that they will be rejected by family and friends and outcast from society. Many of them end up in AIDS "wards" in the countryside, abandoned by their families, and tended only by a few nurses, foreign volunteers, and some Thai helpers who are HIV positive themselves. Manorom sends workers and doctors out to these scattered communities, bringing both drugs and Bibles, nursing skills and friendship, and hope and new life to the patients.

As important as the continuing life at the hospital, however, is the work that God has gone on to do in individual lives.

Only a day after she returned to the UK, Eileen Gordon-Smith heard that her son and his whole family were dead. She was stunned by the extent of her sorrow and loss, feeling that it was a prison from which there seemed to be no escape. But in the depths of her storm of grief she became aware of the strength and love of God holding her safely, and saying, "Peace, be still." She was helped by the outpouring of love and prayer from people all over the world. One letter which comforted her said,

> Just think,
> Of stepping on shore and finding it heaven,
> Of taking hold of a hand and finding it God's hand,
> Of breathing new air and finding it celestial air,
> Of feeling invigorated and finding it immortality,
> Of passing from storm and tempest and finding it unknown calm,
> Of waking up and finding it home.

Rosemary Farrington said that whenever she had heard of women who had lost a child, she marvelled at those who could still praise God. She had always been sure that such an experience would devastate her. When Johnny died, she wept many tears for him, but says, "I'm happy that our little one has gone to his reward." She knows that God has enabled her to witness for him in a way she could never have done before, and this in itself has helped to heal the wounds.

Bryan Parry continued to work at Manorom until 1982, when he returned to New Zealand so that Matthew could begin secondary education. There he met and married Susan, a gastroenterologist, and they now have two more children, Stephen and Sarah. He affirms the truth that God has provided "oil of gladness instead of mourning, and a garment of praise instead of a spirit of despair". He marvels that God was able to bring him out of the depths of his loss to a new life and willingness to love again. He is now Professor and Head of Surgery in the School of Medicine and Health Science at the University of Auckland. He says: "I am different now. I no longer fear death."

All the survivors continued to work for God

in the mission field. It is almost unbearable to think of their pain as they held the broken bodies of their children, their friends and their wives. And yet they came through this time with a kind of glory about them, for their love was undiminished and their faith was strong, and they seem to have been protected – not from sorrow or grief or injury, but from bitterness, resentment and anger. Instead, by a miracle of God's grace, they went on serving the Thai people, bringing them the good news of a Saviour who died for them and transformed life into joy, and death into the assurance of eternal life.

ENGLISH-SPEAKING OMF CENTRES

AUSTRALIA: P.O. Box 849, Epping, NSW 2121
Freecall 1 800 227 154
email: omf-australia@omf.net *www.au.omf.org*

CANADA: 5759 Coopers Avenue, Mississauga ON,
L4Z 1R9
Toll free 1-888-657-8010
email: omfcanada@omf.ca *www.ca.omf.org*

HONG KONG: P.O. Box 70505, Kowloon
Central Post Office, Hong Kong
email: hk@omf.net *www.omf.org.hk*

MALAYSIA: 3A Jalan Nipah, off Jalan Ampang,
55000, Kuala Lumpur
email: my@omf.net *www.omf.org*

NEW ZEALAND: P.O. Box 10-159, Auckland
Tel 09-630 5778   email: omfnz@compuserve.com
www.nz.omf.org

PHILIPPINES: 900 Commonwealth Avenue,
Diliman, 1101 Quezon City
email: ph-hc@omf.net *www.omf.org*

SINGAPORE: 2 Cluny Road, Singapore 259570
email: sno@omf.net *www.omf.org*

SOUTHERN AFRICA: P.O. Box 3080,
Pinegowrie, 2123
email: za@omf.net *www.za.omf.org*

UK: Station Approach, Borough Green, Sevenoaks,
Kent, TN15 8BG
Tel: 01732 887299 email: omf@omf.org.uk
www.omf.org.uk

USA: 10 West Dry Creek Circle, Littleton, CO
80120-4413
Toll Free 1-800-422-5330 email: omf@omf.org
www.us.omf.org

OMF International Headquarters:
2 Cluny Road, Singapore 259570